Wayword

poems by

Anna Polonyi

Finishing Line Press
Georgetown, Kentucky

Wayword

Copyright © 2017 by Anna Polonyi
ISBN 978-1-63534-154-6 First Edition
All rights reserved under International and Pan-American Copyright Conventions.
No part of this book may be reproduced in any manner whatsoever without written permission from the publisher, except in the case of brief quotations embodied in critical articles and reviews.

ACKNOWLEDGMENTS

Grateful acknowledgments to the editors of the journals in which some of these poems first appeared:
Belleville Park Pages: "Tapia"
Paris Lit Up: "Roxica", "Boimorto"
Panorama: The Journal of Intelligent Travel: "Santiago"

Publisher: Leah Maines

Editor: Christen Kincaid

Cover Art: https://stock.adobe.com/license-terms

Author Photo: Richard Beban

Cover Design: Kalman Gacs

Printed in the USA on acid-free paper.
Order online: www.finishinglinepress.com
   also available on amazon.com

Author inquiries and mail orders:
Finishing Line Press
P. O. Box 1626
Georgetown, Kentucky 40324
U. S. A.

Table of Contents

Llanes 1
Ribadesella 2
La Isla 3
La Llamarga 4
Gijón 5
Avilés 6
San Esteban 8
Playa de Xilo 9
Soto de Luña 10
Cadavedo 11
Luarca 12
Piñera 13
Tapia 14
Ribadeo 15
Lourenzá 16
O Bisonte 17
Abadín 18
Vilalba 19
Baamonde 20
Roxica 21
Sobrado 22
Boimorto 23
Arco o Pino 24
Santiago 25
Notes 27

*To all those for whom
eternity is a pot of boiled water waiting to cool*

LLANES

Someone dries their hair in a towel.
        Emerging from the wet, she says,
            "We are all on our own."
                In life, I think she means,
                    but she is talking of the road
                        and how I can claim any bed still empty.

RIBADESELLA

The fish under the bridge
look flat

and dead
until they catch the sun

and hurl it back.
My muscles individually

announce their pain:
wishing to express

common regret at the sudden
change in management,

they will now turn to stone
turn to it for comfort,

for grace as I turn to the wall,
the sea turns into

a highway, the seagull:
a baby.

My bones are loose
and light like the tampons

from a Ziploc bag
the woman on the bottom bunk

hands me, saying:
"I won't need them.

I don't want them
to weigh me down."

LA ISLA

A gull pecks at a fish   cast up on the shore.
It drags the carcass   further out of the waves,
tail first, head heavy   facing the sea.
The gull senses me   watching.
It drops its prize   walks away, not too far,
waits for me   to lose interest,
containing   its excitement,
hoping   to trick me into
thinking   what it found
is of no   value so I will go.
But little   does it know, just as I
did not quite   know until I watch it
watching me   from one side of its head,
that I am unlike   the rest of my species
on this beach: I am a pilgrim, meaning:
I have nowhere   to be but here and that leaves
plenty of time   to watch the gulls,
especially   this one and wait for it
to grow tired   of watching me.

LA LLAMARGA

The last they heard of her was somewhere between Ribadesella and Villaviciosa, when she crossed paths with a German pilgrim who had just finished eating a banana and was about to throw the peel into the eucalyptus forest when she said: "Bananas aren't indigenous to Northern Spain, you know," by which she meant that even if theoretically biodegradable, the banana peel, thrown by his unwitting hand, would stay to alter the Northern Camino landscape. "The next town is another 30 kilometers away," he said, by which he meant it was too far to walk with a banana peel dangling from one hand. To this she replied that she had seen signs to an Albergue only an hour's walk west. With that she was off, the towel tied to her bag swinging with doggish excitement. The German pilgrim never saw any signs, nor did he see her again. (He threw his banana peel into the forest.) Later reports revealed there was indeed an Albergue nearby, opened quite recently by a widow not of these parts. Her name was Rosa but to set her apart from all the other Rosas, they called her Rosa del Flor—she was fond of capuccinas, those yellow-orange flowers that grew in her garden. She would put them in salads and her hair and rave about their virtues to whoever would listen but no one did or else they would have noticed that she never mentioned what those virtues in fact were. They tracked down an Italian with a rose tattoo on his right forearm. He had been one of Rosa's first guests. He came forward wild-eyed and babbling in a Northern Italian accent it took days to place and weeks to decipher. Even then, his testimony was hardly coherent: he spoke of Rosa del Flor—the white widow he called her—and her loyal servant, the dog. (Rosa claimed she had never had a dog.) It seemed he occasionally thought he was her dog, admitting with red cheeks and a tremulous voice that he liked to eat the flowers in her garden straight off of their stems, to sniff out her guests' urine and to masturbate before falling asleep every night, no matter who was in the room. When asked about that specific night however, he wouldn't tell. He just shook his head and murmured the name of the disappeared girl, saying: che peccato, again and again.

GIJÓN

Four men in a bungalow:
        the first jerks off when he thinks the others are asleep;
the second snores like dry thunder;
        the third takes sleeping pills
("that and earplugs, every night!");
        the fourth lets gas until the break of day.
        5:39am.
           I stumble out.

AVILÉS

The city lurches,
    spills its acrid waste,
    heaves itself on top of
        a squirming country cottage,
        caught between a disused highway and a dump.

The sky iron-red
    hovers over a lone tree.
    In its shade: a Turkish pilgrim
        in need of love and water.
        I give her the latter,

keen to eat my cherries and go,
    prise myself loose
    from Gijón's clutches:
        its clattering factories, ravenous asphalt,
        dandelions flaccid with smoke.

My feet scare off crickets
    larger than the lies
    we tell ourselves
        when we sit together
        and sigh.

There is nothing
    like treading lightly
    on this good earth
        bearing nothing
        but what you can carry away.

I have aged a lifetime trying to exit this city.
    The dust I kick up
    cakes my skin white.
        I measure distance in cherry pits,
        spitting them out,

always ahead, so I may have something
      to catch up with
      and the pleasure
            of leaving something behind.

SAN ESTEBAN

Bueno Camino, calls a man,
wishing us a fair spiritual journey
as he zips up his pants
on his way back from the outhouse.

A woman, overweight,
creaks uphill on a fold-up bike.
A shopping bag hanging from the handlebars,
A vacant expression on her face.

Impression being the world pushing itself onto you.
Expression something pushing outward from within.
Either way, there is a lot of push and pull.

Over the tracks no trains have used for years,
the bag swings breathless back and forth.
The woman circles as she cycles.

PLAYA DE XILO

SOTO DE LUÑA

The seagull watches the ocean

for hints of shadow

that are not its own.

Sometimes,

just before nightfall,

it catches itself thinking:

"I am prey."

CADAVEDO
for Bego

The largest storm to have marked these years bears the name of a woman.
Sometimes we call her penance. Sometimes we call her luxury.
Like the strawberries growing on the side of the road,
I learned to live off of exhaust fumes and sunshine,
bracing myself for the backlash of passing forces
larger than myself.

                    The wind, a great invisible hand,
pries us open and fondles us like the long blades of grass
running wild in the fields and washing up against the village.
The men inside watch the cafe sunbrella topple.
They do not move. The cliff they grew up with fell into the sea;
They emerged unscathed but reassembled in a slightly different
configuration.

LUARCA

> *Our regulares have shown the red cowards what it means to be a man. And, incidentally the wives of reds too. Communist and Anarchist women, after all, have made themselves fair game by their doctrine of free love. And now they have at least the acquaintance of real men, not milksops of militiamen. Kicking their legs about and struggling won't save them.*
> —Gonzalo Queipo de Llano (1875-1951), military leader in the Spanish Civil War.

Regulares, I discovered you by accident. Somewhere between Cadavedo and Luarca, my shoelaces came undone. Tying them, I caught sight through the trees of a high, brick wall and a gate in the shape of an onion bulb. An old man with a walking stick called to me from the road.

"Are you lost?" he asked.

"No," I said, "I am just curious."

He lead the way into the parcel of land. There was nothing to see except ferns. "This was a Muslim cemetery. Moroccans are buried here." The man tapped a slab of rock jutting out of the ground. "Franco, you know Franco? He brought them over for the Civil War."

Regulares, you came, tens of thousands, from the Berber desert, to be used as a weapon of war. Whoever wrote the history books left you out, just as they left you in the soil while they dug up their own. A free-loving, free-moving lover of milksops and women, I step over your loose bones. You are now fair game. Struggling didn't save you. Both wronged and wronging, victim and rapist—you, of all people, must have known the dark and light business of being man.

PIÑERA

                                     The   fly says:

         I   murder the heat
                                          slice   through it
                 own
everything   momentarily
          your   foot
                               your   sleeping bag
   your   eyebrow
       your foot   again
     my   patience
                                         is like
the snails'
          outside,
                          clamped down
        on the sun
            -soaked wall
         racing up   to the sky.

TAPIA

I ask the man in the café what the shelter was
                before it was a shelter.
                                  A slaughterhouse, he says.
    The stone is stone-cold, the grass grass-wet
        The fog fills the children's mouths
                          and eats their hair.
            The pink above seeps out
              leaving barely enough
                        for the entire sky.
    Lying on the stone to avoid the grass
        I feel the way prey feels
                      as it is about to become prey.
        I only tell one other person
      (about the slaughterhouse that is,
                    not the sky)

RIBADEO

The woman with the bad leg
from San Pelayo
      shares what is left of the shade:
            she, resting from crossing the square
            me, resting from crossing the country.

    "You are young," she says.
    "You go alone," she says.
"Pray for me when you get there."
She puts her palms together and shakes them at the sky.

The smell of smoke from the village fair clings to me
like the woman's eyes
      as I leave them behind,
      lacking the courage to tell her I don't pray,
      though I walk to the place that may heal her bad leg
      and make me more than a stranger to mine.

LOURENZA

On the path ahead, a matter of life or death.

A frog leaps.

Gliding after it, a snake.

    Both straining,

        at full speed.

            Both

                  unbelievably

                        slow.

O BISONTE
    to Carmela

"Most canvases start off white
but I choose to paint mine black," she says
and layers on the shapes of clouds and leaves
and women in large skirts squatting with surprising ease

like when she drinks from an old Spanish keg
and water escapes from her mouth and runs down her neck.
The collar of her stained shirt blooms dark with wet;
the nipples on her braless breasts turn hard.

She ignores them, wipes her mouth with the back of her wrist.
"Black is so much harder to conquer," she says.

ABADÍN

Doubt says:
I am the sky above and the clouds set hard like bolts in rust;
I am the seagulls pounded by wind;
the telephone wires racing above you;
the last piece of chocolate you offer someone else;
the cigarette butt unsavory as soon as it is no longer lit.
I am what keeps you from getting lost.
I am roughly a kilometer long.
Sometimes you won't need me all day.
But I will lick the blisters off your feet,
peel the tender skin rubbed raw
by rocks and socks, curl around your ankles,
brush the stubble on your legs,
leave kisses in the underside of your knees,
push against the inside of your breasts,
hard with unpregnancy. I am inside your lungs now,
sloshing in the left-overs of your breath.
Should you not have turned left back there?
Are you sure this is the right way?
That's right: take out your map, check again.

VILALBA

                        The eucalyptus says:
Here I am, the infantry,
                        shedding my dress
                        with every turn,
     whiskers curling
       with the heat.
                        Skin me, sun,
              not once
              not twice
                        but every day.
                        Leave my bark stripped
                        bare,
        hanging cheap
like yesterday's clothes
                        over strangers' arms
                        and in return,
     I will give mankind
          my flesh
                        to pierce reckless-silly
                        with inky nibs,
      to finger, unfold
          and seal.

BAAMONDE

What you cannot see:
    elbow, back, neck, ass, mouth, ears, eyes
What you cannot touch:
    back
What you cannot taste:
    elbows, back, neck, ass, ears, eyes, stomach, clit
What you cannot hear:
    muscles building, back sweating,
    bruises blooming, skin burning, nails growing
What you cannot see nor touch nor taste nor hear:
    your back, the mystic of your days.

ROXICA

Somewhere between my underwear and my hipbone,
something has died.
Most things that walk on me
do not leave themselves,
only their absence
and this I have learned not to scratch
but scratch around
with nails grown long and dark with dust.
This one burrows deep
where even I can't follow.
I fold in half,
and see that I am, among many other things,
a place called home.
The man whose tweezers I borrow
offers to help but no, this
is a private duel
between you and me:
Yield, I say, but for god's sake, do not lose your head.

SOBRADO

            The algae of Sobrado says:
    I did not know I was alone   until the scientists said so
cooking I was,
                      in the microscope-glare
  Nitella Flexilis they said,   how odd,
     unheard of   in the whole Iberian peninsula.
              The lily pads—
   I watch them   multiply   like a thousand
green moons.
       The flies   live out their reckless lives.
                      The frogs
catch them,   slipping
            from their lily pads   into the water
   like small mistakes.
Paradise today
       is much the same   as it was some centuries ago,
                  except   perhaps
   for the weeds   choking the church bell's tongue
                            and the cupid's
        broken fingers.

BOIMORTO

I am not immune
    to the charms of women or men:
the curve of an arm,
    the fall of a shirt,
      white teeth
        and my body rustles awake
like leaves in the fall wind.
    My skin touched only by the sun
      that settles whenever I shift
and the sleeping bag
    in the night
      like a slow exhale
        on my body.

ARCA O PINO

A spider crawls out of my sweater's neck,
                                        tries to crawl back into my mouth.

The moths, garish when in motion,
                          are beautiful when set.

The dogs guarding shuttered houses
                        bark mad at the blood leaking from inside me.

In the end, the lizards
            no longer scatter.

They too
    have had to set aside what must be had
from what can be done without.

SANTIAGO

The yellow marks along a curb,
on the back of a garden wall
will only take you so far
I don't know where you are,
only that you follow the same signs
to the land's end and back.
I know what rocks you step on
what rivers you cross
what skies hover above you
because I have seen them too.
We are bound to meet if I stop
and you keep going or you stop
and I keep going—
I just don't know which.
So in years to come,
I'll keep an eye out
for the color yellow.
It may yet lead me to you
or you to me
or us both to all the others
we lost somewhere along the way.

NOTES

These poems were written on the road during a pilgrimage along the northern coast of Spain to Santiago de Compostel. The title of each poem refers to the town, village or shelter where I stayed for the night.

"Sobrado": Sobrado's lagoon, built by monks in the 16th century, contains a type of algae that, when detected in 1980, was thought to be the only one of its kind on the Iberian Peninsula. Since then, *Nitella Flexilis* has also been found in other parts of Spain, but the signage at the lagoon claiming exclusivity has yet to be updated.

"Luarca": The quote is drawn from Paul Preston's *The Spanish Civil War: Reaction, Revolution and Revenge*. Regulares, or Moroccan mercenaries enlisted by force to fight opponents of Franco in exchange for promises of payment, remain a relatively unexplored subject in contemporary Spanish history. Many of the fallen Moroccan soldiers were left unidentified during later exhumations.

"Vilalba": The presence of eucalyptus trees in Galicia is the subject of some controversy. Planted mostly in the post-war era, they are considered to be an invasive species but due to the tree's rapid growth compared to indigenous varieties, it has been favored by the government for the production of paper.

ADDITIONAL ACKNOWLEDGMENTS

I am grateful to my teachers: Joanna Klink and Jorie Graham and to the community of writers who have supported me with seemingly endless generosity here in Paris. Thank you to Kaaren Kitchell in particular for getting me to sit down and submit my work.

Alina Mogilyanskaya, Alex Manthei, Carole Cassier and Linda Healey were my early readers and had the generosity of spirit to imagine the poems in their ideal form. Thank you to the editors at Radio France Internationale whose interest in the pilgrimage helped fund it and to Marcelle Balt for joining me at the end of the Earth.

I am deeply thankful for all those who helped make this chapbook possible: A. Janoshazi, X. Richert, D. Kitchen, S. Petrusz, J. Henderson, J. Charles, D. Thomas, M. Woods, E. Stern, F. Veress, E. Lupine, L. Heyer, G. Wald, F. Pongor, S. Hunsucker, A. Somjen, L. Khalifah, D. Mazurkevich, M. Vassileva, R. Hughes, T. Hughes, E. Jakim, L. Estus, J. Connell, M. Hinzmann, L. Gellman, J. Galinato, O. Simons, H. Latty-Mann.

Special thanks to Richard Beban for the headshot and Kalman Gacs, who designed the cover with speed and grace.

Last but definitely not least: Ultreya to all pilgrims, pilgrims to-be and to the kind people who gave us shelter along the way.

Anna Polonyi is a Franco-American-Hungarian poet, writer and journalist. Born to Hungarian parents in Boston, MA, she grew up in Strasbourg, France. A Harvard graduate, she is the former recipient of a Fulbright fellowship and the 2015 Sylvia Beach Short Fiction Prize. She holds a Master's degree from Sciences Po Paris and her journalistic work has appeared with *The New York Times*, *The Washington Post*, *Foreign Policy*, *Radio France Internationale*, *The Irish Times*, *Times of India*, *Die Tageszeitung*, *The European*, amongst others. *Wayword* is her first chapbook. She lives in Paris, France.

www.ingramcontent.com/pod-product-compliance
Lightning Source LLC
LaVergne TN
LVHW041514070426
835507LV00012B/1568